T0290385

SIERRA STEPHENSON

A Rose THAT GREW FROM CONCRETE

A Rose That Grew From Concrete
© 2022 Sierra Stephenson

All rights reserved. This book or any portion thereof may
not be reproduced or used in any manner whatsoever
without the express written permission of the publisher
except for the use of brief quotations in a book review.

Print ISBN: 978-1-66784-500-5
eBook ISBN: 978-1-66784-501-2

Prologue for Book

Life has been a roller coaster with a whole lot of ups and downs.. granted my childhood was wonderful until the year 2007. My mother provided, installed and nurtured her children all 4 of us. We never wanted for anything in this world. At the age of 18 my mom had all 4 of us including her 2 brothers to support. My mom was the strongest woman I've ever met. She didn't back down from anything. I've never seen her hurt until the day my grandmother passed away in February 2007. That was the day my life changed as well. My brother and I found my grandmother dead in the bathroom of our home, however I never really got to grieve over her. I believe at a young age I was able to accept death for what it was! My mom had changed so much after this and was hurting from the inside that it began to show on her outside. Her father had also passed away a few months before my grandmother, she was in this cold world without both of her parents. She was very close with her parents, this has caused lots of depression. My grandmother helped my mother raise us. After she passed away our family started to spread apart but my mother kept us all together, that was until the day she passed away. My mother was brutally murdered by her husband on December 25th of 2007. 10 months after her mother passed away, a year after her father passed away.... she was killed by gun violence, her husband Andrew Wells suffered from severe depression. He committed a homicide,suicide. My older siblings walked in and found them both breathless christmas morning. This late night, early morning is one I'd never forget. The night before my mom was at work and we spoke before her shift started about the gifts I received for christmas. I got one gift less than what I wanted and she wasn't able to afford it.. she mentioned that money didn't grow on trees.She told me she'll call me after work and told me love you, that was the last time I spoke to

1

my mother. I kept calling her phone after 11pm because I knew she was off but didn't get a response. Later that night my cell kept ringing with my family, calling to check up on me and right away I knew something wasn't right. Finally one of my cousins called and told me what had happened to my mother. That night the lord had already given me a gift of discernment, I knew what happened to my mother before she could even say anything. I had kept calling my step father's phone but I didn't get an answer. I left voicemails and sent text messages. That night I also received the spirit of forgiveness which I never knew was possible to do such a thing right away. Years later my family still dealt with much heartache and pain after losing two really important people in our lives, it was more than traumatic. My family became divided and in the summer of 2008 my brother and I were shipped away to live with my aunt in Des Moines, Iowa. That was when things began to really change in my life. I became wild, started to smoke weed and cigarettes, drink, have sex, stealing and lying, going to adult night clubs, driving cars under age, anything I wanted to do I did. I didn't have the correct guidance because my aunt was always at work to make sure we had a roof over our head and food in our mouths. I got sucked into the wrong crowd and became lost. I moved back to Minnesota and started exotic dancing, having sex for money when needed, popping pills and sleeping with women. I had completely let myself go. I want to thank God for installing a drive in me to keep going forward in school. I was able to graduate high school because doing things that were productive made me feel whole. I felt important and worth more than what I had become. Eventually I moved in with my father, we didn't really see eye to eye because I didn't accept who he was and what he was doing, not realizing that I was doing the same thing, drinking and doing drugs. He made sure we had a roof over our head and provided. He showed tough love because that's all he knew. The relationship that me and my father shared was bitter sweet but overall the love is unconditional. We just couldn't live in the same home because I thought I was grown. A couple years later I moved to Marietta, Georgia with my oldest sister and her children. When I moved to GA that was the happiest moment for me in many years. I stayed for a few months until her relationship with a man began to take a turn to seriousness and I was very uncomfortable with her situation due to what has happened to my mother in the past.. She did tell me I could always go back home if that would make me feel better and that's exactly what I did. Once I made it back to Minnesota, I signed up for college, got a job and found a one bedroom apartment. This was the year I conceived my son Harlem. Harlem father and I were good friends growing up, I had gone with his cousin before we started dating but the guy kept going to jail. Harlem father always had a crush on me but I never looked at him in such a way until one night. He came over and we had a few drinks.. One thing led to another and 9 months later a child was born. I had gone through many things with this man but I took it as being punished because I was out of God's will while living in sin. Time passed and we split up. I moved on with my life after giving birth to my child, depression and anxiety came on strong. A few years later my sister, my best friend, my biggest supporter had passed away due to a heart attack at a very young age. She has been my God sister for 16 years, this death has hit me pretty hard, I wasn't ready for what happened, I couldn't handle what I was faced with for a very long time. I had to do something about my situation so I decided to move away. I moved to Saint Cloud, Mn where I found quite affordable housing and many opportunities here. If I didn't know how to do something, I sure learned how to after moving away alone. I began to work as a Nursing Assistant full time, I pulled doubles and triples in order to make sure Harlem and I didn't need or want for anything, we lived a really good life by the grace of God. December 29th 2019 my brother caught a case here in Stearns County. It's been 2 years since he's been in jail... After he went to jail 9 months later I moved back to Minneapolis.... Once I moved back to Minneapolis I was blessed with a Job at a hospital and worked there for 2 months. I went on vacation to Florida and I let go of my job. God has been providing for my household for 2 years without stable income. During the month of January I began my first fast, it lasted for 5 days, my second fast was on February 16th-26th for 10 days. I had completed it and also received a breakthrough, a cleansed heart and the holy spirit. The fast caused me to feel light as a feather. March 09th 2021 I got pregnant out of God's will.. I became depressed for 8 weeks straight because I had made a covenant to God and broke it because I wasn't fully prepared for enemy attacks. I got pregnant by a person that wasn't a man of God, I really didn't know much about him at the time... This time I had fallen off track for a bit and wasn't in my word for about 3 weeks that had put a void in my walk with God. 3 months later I was able to get back to the level of comfort that I had with God, rebuild where I had forfeited. This season I had been in spiritual warfare at an all time high. The enemy tries to attack at every angle. I had been tested by God on my faith, I lost both of my cars, I was in a car accident, I had a few different health issues, but through it all I gave it to God. I was able to allow him to work through me no matter what situation I was faced with in my life. Through it all I was still able to give God his glory. God had also isolated me so I can sit still and pay attention to his ways and become obedient. During this time I was able to trust in God, accept things that I once didn't, become more humble, pay attention, be more grateful, I learned to appreciate the small things in life. I was able to spend time and dwell in the presence of the Lord, grow closer to him and his word. God had begun to strip me of things that didn't serve and have purpose to the Kingdom. Now I am currently back in Saint Cloud, MN as of September 2021. I am 31 weeks pregnant and living in a better situation, I moved back for one reason and that's to fight for my brother's case where he was wrongfully convicted. I am also on my 3rd fast and boy has it been a journey. During these past couple weeks God has revealed many things to me through my spirit. He will continuously be with me and my children through the rest of our lives. I just want to thank God for all the things he has done in me and my children's lives. Bringing me out of a lost dark place, delivering me from evil. He has completely transformed me inside, out. The things that you are about to read are going to blow your mind, God has been completely working in my life, the things he's done and the things he's said , the things he's approved and the things he's denied, God has revealed many things about my life and who he has created me to be. This book will teach you how to grow closer to God and how to rebuke the enemy out of your life. Learning how to pray for breakthroughs and become the woman God has called you to be...No matter how big the problem, God is Bigger, Stronger And Better.. You'll learn how to pray and become obedient to God's will

Being Deceived By The Enemy

I left Minnesota and moved to Des moines, Iowa with both of my children . we left everything behind, I believed that God told me to give everything away and go.. It was only a few things God told me to bring with me. As soon as I made it to Iowa, I was spiritually and mentally attacked. I was being mentally abused by the enemy. I had been a prisoner in my own mind. One night I heard a whisper in my ear, New Life. I looked it up and it was a Church. I started to go on Sunday and Wednesday services. The days I went it felt like the message was just for me. I believed God sent me there , I had been hearing voices and being completely tormented in my sleep as well, I had even begun to be physically abused. I started to become scared to pray and open my bible. I because terrorized and trumatized , I even started to hide my face from the Lord because I had started to thing that I was letting God down and he was upset with me because I was experienceing so many things. I honestly felt as if God's wrath was on my life. I thought God had taken his hand off of my life. I literally thought my life was completely over. I had begun to start reaching out to people, all kinds of people, people I thought were from God, of God , sent by God, just to hear from God. I was seeking everyone but God. The enemy kept whispering in my ear that I will betray God. I couldn't believe that I allowed the enemy to get in my space and mind. People started to take advantage of me because they noticed that I was feeling lost and confused. I even started watching youtube videos to get a word from God. It was bad that I couldn't understand or hear his voice this season. It was very confusing and disappointing. I didn't realize that I was speaking word curses over my own life. The thing I was speaking about had started to manifest. In the bible it says what a man thinks he is. I had become disobedient to God in this season. I don't know why and for some reason I felt like I needed help to become obedient. I had never experienced anything like this before. It was the worst season of my life. God would answer me and I still would ask someone else to get the answer. People saw my weakness and they started speaking things over me as well. I had started to be called witches., Certain things started to happen to me. It was like the devil was trying to steal my soul. It was a battle for my soul. I was dealing with all kinds of spirits. The spirit of sudicide, a spiritual husband I had married thinking God was asking me to be his bride, maman, depression, anxiety,The spirit of confusion and deceitfulness. A spirit of religion tried to jump off on me. I had even thought God was telling me to join this Church in Iowa. I was driving past the Church and I believed I heard God tell me to stop at this Church, so I did. It said Apostilic on there and I remember during my pregnancy that I got a word about Apostilic Pentecost... So when I saw the building I stopped. When I got out of the car I saw this man holding a gun on his hip and I felt some kind of way but I didn't listen to the Holy Spirit inside of me. I spoke with everyone that was there and was accepted with open arms. The Church was big and beautiful with royal blue suede seats and the pool pit was really nice with gold trimming. As I spoke with the member and broke down I caught the Holy Ghost. They all started to say how they felt the power of God inside of the building. I thought I was being led to my home Church and I joined and got baptized. As I got to the back, I started to feel super weird. I was confused about the way I was feeling. They started to ask questions and I didn't know what I was feeling. I knew I believed in Jesus but when they asked me before getting in the water I felt like I didn't believe. I was scared to get into and was pressured into the water. After I got out of the water I started to see and feel out of my element, they started putting their hands on me, It was five men and women. They kept asking me do you hear someone speaking in tongues? Did you catch the holy ghost? They were trying to get me to believe that I had caught the holy spirit. The Holy Spirit was already inside of me, God was already inside of me. They jumped up and ran into the corner. They start looking at me as if I was crazy. I saw the devil on those people. They had manipulated me again and told me I was just nervous and what had just happened was a life changing experience . I stood in front of the mirror and saw the glow of God on me but once again I started to notice something didn't feel right. The next day I went back to the so-called Church and before I left the house I heard the Holy Spirit say Cult, But I thought it was just a voice that I had been traumatized by. I met the Pastor and his office was so huge and well put together, It wasn't a regular Pastor office. Again I thought it was the enemy trying to stop me from going to worship. Soon as I walked into the Church I felt that weird uneasy feeling again and as I tried worshiping God I was being attacked by the spirit in that place. There were ladies in the place that started praying for me and I was looking at them having the thought of them being a witch. As the lady was putting her hand on my head praying for me, it felt like she was stealing the power and gifts God had given me. I was praying, screaming, on the floor and begging God to help me. She was taking my strength from me and I started to feel defeated. When the Pastor came into the place he invited me into his space and we spoke, he looked evil in his face, in his eyes, in his smile. As we spoke I could see that everything I was experiencing wasn't for anything I was in the wrong place, I had been invited there by the enemy. After answering his questions, I was leaving out and looking down on his desk. I noticed a book that said the illuminati. it was in plain sight, he wasn't trying to hide it either. That told me that many people in the Church knew what was already taking place in the Church. As I stepped into the lobby of the church I looked around and realized that I have seen this place before in a dream. It felt as if I was standing in the lobby of hell. God had tried giving me warning prior. As I was waiting on my ride to leave this lady had said God told her to give me some money. These other ladies came and offered me dinner. So once again I started to get confused,

So we went and as I was sitting in the car with these two ladies I started to see the spirit on them and I noticed that they didn't have the fruit of the spirit.. The things they were saying and how they conducted themselves. The way they were talking, judging people, gossiping and so much more. That was it... God had completely opened my eyes as we left .. I changed my phone number and never went back to that place again. A week later I had got delivered from the spirits that had been attaching themselves to me and right after that I heard, Dallas Texas. Remind you I thought God sent me to Iowa.. I heard danger, wait to leave until Monday, but nope I left that friday. That weekend I saw so many things on the road. It was people drug/ sex trafficking. It felt very off and uncomfortable, so I made small talk to people in the bus station like mothers and couples. As we entered KC, Mossori I noticed many things happening where I couldn't get on not one but 2 buses going to Texas. During this trip my discernement kicked in. I had even seen someone that was practicing witchcraft. I asked the manager to sit in the security office. I saw things that I once would've never seen. It was as if everyone was watching me. The enemy has agents and they are out here working. I decided to stay in KC for the night because I just didn't feel right getting on that bus ... I was dealing with the spirit of fear. The bus station closed at 1am. I had found a safe place for me to sleep until the next morning. The next morning our ride to Texas went really well, the same people that were in KC drug trafficking were on that same bus when we made it to Texas. At a stop I saw six men get off the bus and stand in my space staring me down... If looks could kill i'd be dead. I figured they had discussed what had happened the night before with me and the things that started taking place. The whole time in Dallas I kept hearing about death. I didn't know if they thought I was going to call the police on them or the FBI but I wanted to mind my business. AS we got to the bus station The men were looking around and checking the area to see if they had the green light to keep going, that wasn't my place to tell them because my safety is important. I never saw drugs but it was in my spirit. I had a relative pick me up from the bus station and I stayed with her for about 3 weeks. Everyone looked so suspicious and was so on edge. It was the truth but also because of the experiences that I had in Iowa. I kept thinking and speaking the blood of Jesus because I knew that God covers me. I had been living in fear and I didn't realize that it started taking control. My relative had opened her doors to me and I tried to stay but my spirit wasn't settled. It truly was a beautiful city and home. That still wasn't enough, I had something trying to hold me back from worshiping and going deeper with God. I didn't want to let God down, so I tried to stick it out and stay. I kept hearing Dallas so it went to the shelter, once again it wasn't from God. I wasn't supposed to be there. I had to lie in order to get in the shelter so I knew that wasn't God. One day I spoke to my sister and she read a verse from her daily scripture and it was God speaking through his word. I received my answer. I could go home ... He had never sent me out.. Yes he told me to move but It wasn't stated.. It was to move out of the home that I was currently in before I moved to Iowa. It was a journey that I had been on.. It was a test... Time was up in that season, I had got on the greyhound to go back home. I had learned the lesson God wanted me to and that was to have discernment and not the enemy miles away , I learned his ways, his tactics and schemes.. His plots and plans... As I got on the bus to go back home I got attacked so badly in my mind. I still was somewhat confused about my direction. I didn't know if God was upset with me because of the lack of knowledge and understanding I had. During the last couple hours of my ride, I had got on the prayer line and after I got offline, I had a wild thought. It was like I instantly felt a relief as if a weight was lifted. I felt a sense of peace. I have never felt something being broken off of me the way that it had been. I didn't only deal with the mental battles and physical health issues.. I was on the verge of a mental crisis . I almost gave up on my faith, my future , my destiny and my family. That night Jesus came and spoke to me saying how important it was for me to keep pushing, many people need to hear this story because it'll help someone . People will realize that they can get through the attacks of the enemy, people can receive breakthroughs, the deliverance and strength. The devil wanted me to stop walking, stop believing, he wanted me to stop having faith, he wanted me to stop fighting, he wanted me to lose hope, he wanted me to stay down and stay low, stay out of the bible and stop going into prayer... But let me tell you how good God is.. God is amazing, he will bring you up and out of the pit, he will bring you out of that dark place, he will catch you before you fall, God will help you stand tall, he will give you strength in your weakest moment. He will send peace and love to you and feel lonely, when you are feeling unloved. When you are going through that tough time, that time that seems like death is near, that time when it seems like it won't and can get better just know that things will and can turn around for your goodness. You have to keep speaking to your situation, keep speaking love and life into your situation... The enemy couldn't get to me anymore so he started to send people that I love. They told me they'd kill me and said hateful things to me but my God is a strong tower. I wasn't worried he gave me visions even before some of these things were going to take place but that's not to worry about because God is in control of the situation... No matter what situation you're faced with, just stand firm and keep going. Anything is possible with God.

God strength during the attacks

Receiving healing from The Lord has been one of the most amazing experiences, many times he's showed up and touched my household health. The Lord has done many miracles, signs and wonders I had previously been in and out of the hospital because I dealt with really severe headaches, dizziness, lightheadedness, I felt fatigue as well. I had to go to the neurologist to see what could possibly be causing these issues. My heart had begun to beat funny so I had to wear a heart monitor for 14 days and they noticed my heartbeat was irregular. The cardiologist diagnosed me with a type 2 heart block. As I got off the phone, in my heart I had strong faith knowing once I went back to my appointment I would be healed by stripes on Jesus' back. I went back after finding out the results and was healed, they couldn't find anything wrong. I got into a car crash as well and had to go to physical therapy and chiropractor as well. During this time I had gestational diabetes, having to go to doctor appointments 3-4 times a week while being pregnant, this lasted for 9 whole months. During the birth of my child I had to get an emergency c- section. During that time something didn't feel right, I felt that my wound was infected. I went to the hospital and came to find out they found E coli in my wound. I dealt with anxiety, panic attacks and depression. I fought with many demonic spirits that are out to attack and steal your soul, the enemy is running wild in the world trying to steal, kill and destroy the plans God has for your life. My daughter experienced a demonic attack on her health at 12 days old. She had been admitted into the hospital on the same day she was supposed to be born. I noticed my daughter's breathing was off and I didn't know that my little cousin was playing with witchcraft... I had spent the night over their house for 3-4 days and during that time I noticed my daughter's breathing pattern off, God dropped it in my spirit to take her to the hospital, so I made an appointment at the pediatrician. We made it in and the nursing assistant took vital signs the first time her oxygen was at 93%. About 10-15 minutes later it was at 85% then dropped to 65%. The nurses had to put her on oxygen, The Lord dropped it in my spirit to contact my dear friend, who was also my accountability partner. She answered and God then again dropped it in my spirit to have her call this man of God which is a prophet- minister. He had me ask everyone to be quiet in the room while praying for my daughter, he also said within 30 minutes she'll be breathing at 100% on her own. Within 2 minutes later my sweet baby girl was breathing on her own. We got sent to the ER and there weren't any beds available for infants in the state of Minnesota. 2 hours later the doctor came in and told me that the Children's Hospital in Minneapolis was on their way to transport us for care. She was in the NICU for 5 days, many blood tests and other tests were performed and they all came back negative. By the Grace of God and with the Blood of Jesus covering my child. I thank God for blessing me with my children and protecting us throughout every situation that we face, especially through the storm. This book is based on all true life experiences. God's power is so big and mighty, we humans wouldn't be able to comprehend or imagine because it's too much for our minds. If it wasn't for God's grace and mercy I would not be where I am today.

Being brave during spiritual warfare

Spiritual warfare is nothing to play with, some doors are harder to close, you have to be careful who you allow in your space, home, life ect. No matter how you feel deep down in order to get through this situation you have to be brave and stand firm because the enemy tries to throw the spirit of fear off on people. No matter the attack you have to know that God is with you and you're not alone. Fight the enemy with praise, worship praying with authority while declaring and decreeing in the name of Jesus.! The enemy is always out looking for prey to devour. He looks for the weak and vulnerable. You have to use prayers of protection and keep the scriptures close. It's all about your mindset and how your thought process is. God will strengthen you for this battle, It is a war zone we live in. It is not a game these demons come to attack at a all time high, they don't stop until you get up and cast them back down to the pits of hell, you have to really be firm and take charge of the situation because they can sense fear in the air, they stalk especially around the midnight hour. Sometimes they come as early as 6pm soon as the late evening arrives is when the demonic spirits of darkness comes to terrorize people. These are not just any ole spirit these spirits have authority in the Kingdom of darkness, they are forces of darkness. In order to get rid of them it has to be a serious deliverance with the power of God. The person doing deliverance has to have strong faith praying over you and believe for you deliverance from the demonic spirit that has tried to attach itself. No telling where this came from. It could be from someone that you are or previously dealing with, it could have jumped off someone on to the next. someone could've possibly practiced witchcraft against you... all sorts of things or simply because you are a child of God and are beginning your journey. In your journey with the Lord and the enemy wants to try anything to stop you from furthering your relationship with the Lord. He will also send monitoring spirits to watch your every move to report back to him. He comes to steal, kill and destroy.. With that being said he is the mastermind of creating disease, attacks on people weather it's economic issues, education system failure, even government failures. In order for him to do these things he has to get permission first and honesty. The first thing we should do when this happens is begin to get on our knees and pray to the Lord because he is our refuge, our savior, his name isn't Prince of Peace for nothing. There are many kind of demonic spirits and you have to be very careful because these things will drive you to commit suicide, murder and many other crimes. They are a pon used by the enemy, that's why people deal with mental health, physical and emotional health related issues because it is an attack of the dark world... Most people don't know that they are operating in a dark spirit because they live a worldly life and look at things with a natural eye. Many people don't believe that spiritual attacks a real and the government tries to cover it up with a diagnosis, they send people to mental hospitals and shove medication down these people throaths for speaking about what they are seeing In this world, the health care workers, government workers, and so on know exactly what's going on in this world but they want to keep covering things up not realizing that these things shall come to light very soon. The government wants to push under the rug the real issue and that's that this world is being run in darkness.

Standing up to the Giants

It's easier said than done, the giant is like a fly that keeps bugging you and won't go anywhere. In order to sleigh your giants you have to know its tricks,tactics and ways. The enemy has many devices, schemes, schedules, plots and plans. It's important to know how your opponent operates and the way he/she thinks. See the enemy thinks we'er dumb because some of us are uneduacted when it comes to who we are Christ and what kind of power and authoriy is

behind us. Most people don't know that we have a whole heavenly team waiting to come and shake the earth for us because Our Father isn't going to play about his children period. We have angles that we can send down to protect us, healing angels, guardian angels, angles that fight the warfare, angles that help us get through grieving situations and even to escort us to after life. It doesn't matter how big or small the giant is, you have to fight for your life.

The enemy wants you to shrink back because he's used to people giving up and allowing him to come in and do as he pleases. It doesn't matter how afraid, how scared, how uncomfortable, how worried you are, this is something you have to do with faith. Your faith will cause things to happen, I mean mountains will literally move with the great faith you have deep down inside. You have to fight with the words of the lord but speaking scripture and declaring and decreeing

something with the blood of Jesus and sealing it with the blood. When you are in this battle speak to that giant and make sure you are detailed as you bind up the spirit, things that are hindering or tormenting you. As you bind that thing up, you replace it with the word of God or the peace of God. Denounce the things that you are experiencing and loosening the peace, love, patience and mind of Christ. Make sure to worship, listen to praise music and speak life into the situation whatever the devil says you are or not say reply with the opposite.Just know before it gets better they will turn the heat up on you but don't allow them to take over because they will try to kill you. There is no way to get through this without God and a Christian team that has authority and knows Christ.! It's war, ain't no holding back because these things don't mind who they attack, they want blood, they come for babies, elders, animals, anything alive. It's time to stand up and FIGHT don't hold back go all the way in.You are not alone there are many other people in this world that deal with these situations and many are afraid to ask for help; if that's you please don't be and set your pride to the side to ask for the help you need. The spirits will even have you believing you are good enough to do the thing God has told you to do. You'll feel discouraged and stuck. Unable to get through the situations you're faced with, the enemy's job is to stop you but as long as you have God all things are possible.

Praise through the pain

When we're faced with real life problems and tramatic memories of the past that's created pain, we as humans tend to surpress the feelings or cope with drugs, alcohol, sex or other addictions. These are spirits we've opened ourselves up to not being able to close those doors. It's going to take a lot of praising, worshiping and being delivered from the darkness. We never run to our source, Father God. The light of life. He is the true living God, his words bring forth life. Between the pages of the bible is a map for this journey through life. When you're in a situation experiencing the aftermath of that thing that's continuously holding you back make sure you pray, no it's not easy, it's not fun but that's when you should run to the altar and dwell in the Lord God presence. Reading the word of God will uplift your spirit and build your faith as you fight this battle. You have to dig deep in order to overcome these things. You have to allow God to get into that place and perform the surgery he needs to do in order to heal and put together those broken places. Our hearts may be heavy, they might be empty, they might be hardened or broken.. Our soul may be lowley and could possibly be screaming out for dear life... The love of God brings peace and comfort, past our understanding. The more you praise the more you'll feel a sense of relief. It's been many days that I wanted to give up and crawl under a rock because I didn't understand what I was going through. God will give you the strength to stand tall when you're feeling weak, he will give you comfort when you're feeling down, and he will give you peace when in a chaotic season. God is a man that shall not lie. If he told you he'll do it, that's what he means. Your pain will hold some things up in life, you will not be able to move forward. Your pain will cause you delays and not move forward. It also could cause you to damage others. That trauma will affect the way you trust.

Your thought process and the way you see others. It's up to you to fight for yourself no one else will do it, you can't sit around moping thinking things will change without you taking steps and making moves. That's like the saint's prayers without work means nothing. So if you're reading this now it's time to start your healing journey, focus on your healing and not the pain. We should know that God turns our pain into purpose. He turns our pain into power, that's something that we all have deep within us but we have to dig deep down and pull it out. These small prayers are barely being heard, I'm telling you right now, start digging deep in prayers and pray with authority. Our Lord God has granted each of his children things that no man can take. We have power and treasure deep within. Now is the time to tap into that treasure box and spend quality time with Our Father. He wants a Intimate relationship with his children. If you start now your pain won't be able to hold you, your mind, heart and spirit captive. Once you become set free you won't want to go back. I promise you that, unless you're looking back to remind yourself of how far you've come. There is abundance of love, life, peace, health, freedom and wealth when partnering with our Father God. When faced with distress dwell in the Lord's presence.

Choose life over death

When you come from a bloodline of death, imprisonment and failure it's hard to see anything past death because that's what was seen going up but we all have the choice to choose the right path. When you believe that Jesus is your savior and The Lord God is his father you'll have life but that doesn't mean it's an easy walk because it's not. You have a lot of work to do. Our father wants to spend time with his children, he'll take you through a season of testing to form you into his image, you'll go through much pain and suffering but that's what happens when you are a child of God. We suffer just like Christ had to suffer in this cold world we live in. People love worldly things and ways, materials and money not understanding that when you choose God that your life is just benning and you are saved from death and sin. The Lord wants us to kill our flesh to live and walk the same way Christ did while he was on earth for the 33 years to live. Die to your flesh and become a live in the spirit. They both are always fighting because the flesh doesn't want to bow down and obey the Spirit of Christ, this life is a challenge in the beginning but when you're in and you're serious it won't be hard to obey the Lord because you know that he is your everything. I had no choice but to follow the Lord. It was the only way I could go because I answered the call when the phone rang and he chose me to get some things done in this world before he comes to take us home with him. Our father only wants what's best for his children; he is concerned about everything that has to do with us. I had to pick my cross up and walk because I didn't have any other option. It was life or death for me and I chose life with my father. I don't and won't let him down, the people that are assigned to my ministry or my bloodline. My children, their children and so on depended on it. When walking with Our father things began to get broken off of you and your bloodline but you have to believe and press on. The children and the next generations depend on you to fight through this because no matter the situation they are looking up to you and you want to free the family from curses from our ancestors' past mistakes. When on this journey you have to read your word and feed your spirit with a good message and edifying things. The enemy will try you even more once you decide to give your life to Christ.

God's peace in the midst of the storm

God's word brings peace alone, you have to have faith and know that our Father will never let anything touch you; you are off limits the only thing the enemy can do is try you and if you're not strong enough then you'll fail. Praise dancing helped me, speaking encouraging affirmations to myself in the mirror helped me. Singing gospel music, going to church and being around a community of believers.. whether it was on social media or in person, just being surrounded around positive people that are willing to uplift, speak life and encourage you is very helpful. The Lord has many scriptures in the Bible that'll bring peace to you. The Bible is a map for life, it's instruction on how to live life correctly, I know that sounds weird but for many years I didn't know how to live life because I wasn't taught how. Even though I used to go to Church as a young girl with my GodMother, I still didn't understand.. Most of us are products of our environment but we have the choice not to be. God's love brings real peace.. Peace that suprasses all understanding, I couldn't even understand what I was feeling or experiencing because it was something I never felt before. It was calm, quiet, inside out... I mean my soul was quiet, my mind was still. My mind wasn't racing. It was so unusual that I thought I had made God upset. I literally thought I did something wrong because I wasn't in a battle anymore, I wasn't warning in my mind, I wasn't on defense mode... It was uncomfortable for a while because I wasn't used to having real peace. If you're unsure if you know the love of the Lord then check in your Bible. Raed on the love of God. God's love is shown through actions not words. Every morning he wakes us up with a new mind and new mercy and grace. Do you love your neighbors, do you love your sister's and brother's? Do you move with peace, are you kind? The fruits of the spirit alone and the Lord alone is Love. Peace over evil acts is love. Some examples of the peace of God is a sound mind, quiet spirit, internally you'll feel clear, cleansed and free. Your heart won't be heavy and you will not be in a battle. The Lord is alway and forever in control of everything of this world. We have to allow him to do what he does. No one knows more than our father. Lean on him, lay your burdens down and allow Christ to pick them up.

Walk by faith & not by sight

When we enter a different season in our lives it could be frightening because we don't know what's ahead of us. The journey of life is the unknown. One thing that we all can agree on is The Lord God will always be with us wherever we go. Faith can take you a long way, when your faith is strong and unwavering, you can move mountains. You can cause things to happen in the spirit realm and it causes things to come to life in the natural realm. It isn't easy to keep your faith alive if you're not feeding your spirit with the words of God, listening to uplifting music or being around God's people that speak life and not death. Having faith will bring you right out of that dark place that's trying to hold you prisoner. We might not know where we're going and when we will make it but just know we'll make it to the destination. When walking by faith and not by sight, you have to really trust in the Lord that is when you will be tested because if we are God's children we have to trust in him in all we do. The Lord told me to pack up my children's clothes and give all of my purses, shoes, heels, and clothes away, furniture, kids room sets, beds and so on and move out of state. The Lord was doing a new thing with me.. See this was a test he wanted to make sure I trusted him. It was important for me to move when the Lord told me to move in order to be in the will of God. He wanted to make sure I didn't care more about material than him, he wanted to make sure I was going to obey his commands. Walking by faith means you're obeying the Lord no matter what the situation, circumstance is. No matter what it seems like or feels like. I'm not saying don't acknowledge how you feel or you're now, I'm saying acknowledge it and keep going because in the end you'll realize that those things are there to stop you from moving forward in the things God has called you to do. The enemy wants to stop you from reaching the heaven gates. Walking by faith requires you to believe that the unseen can be reached... What's not seen is what really matters and the things we can see doesn't. The things unseen lasts for eternity, the things seen don't even last a lifetime.. There is no real value in things seen. So that is why we have to trust our Father that he'll bring us through the fire unburnt, he'll bring us through the storm untouched. Faith is the substance of things (unseen) hope for. The thing we as believers need to remember is that God is always with us no matter where we are. We may not be able to see him but as long as you know..!

Scriptures Of Protection

King James Version Holy Bible

Ephesians 6:10-20

Finally, my brethren, be strong in the Lord, and in the power of his might.

Put on the whole armour of God, that ye may be able to stand against the wiles of the devil.

For we wrestle not against flesh and blood, but against principalities, against powers, against the rulers of the darkness of this world, against spiritual wickedness in high places.

Wherefore take unto you the whole armour of God, that ye may be able to withstand in the evil day, and having done all, to stand.

Stand therefore, having your loins girt about with truth, and having on the breastplate of righteousness;

And your feet shod with the preparation of the gospel of peace;

Above all, taking the shield of faith, wherewith ye shall be able to quench all the fiery darts of the wicked.

And take the helmet of salvation, and the sword of the Spirit, which is the word of God:

Praying always with all prayer and supplication in the Spirit, and watching thereunto with all perseverance and supplication for all saints;

And for me, that utterance may be given unto me, that I may open my mouth boldly, to make known the mystery of the gospel,

For which I am an ambassador in bonds: that therein I may speak boldly, as I ought to speak

Joshua 1 :9

Have not I commanded thee? Be strong and of good courage; be not afraid, neither be thou dismayed: for the Lord thy God is with thee whithersoever thou goest.

1 Peter 5:8-11

Be sober, be vigilant; because your adversary the devil, as a roaring lion, walketh about, seeking whom he may devour:

Whom resist steadfast in the faith, knowing that the same afflictions are accomplished in your brethren that are in the world.

But the God of all grace, who hath called us unto his eternal glory by Christ Jesus, after that ye have suffered a while, make you perfect, stablish, strengthen, settle you.

To him be glory and dominion for ever and ever. Amen.

Hebrews 13:20

Now the God of peace, that brought again from the dead our Lord Jesus, that great shepherd of the sheep, through the blood of the everlasting covenant,

Matthew 15:13

But he answered and said, Every plant, which my heavenly Father hath not planted, shall be rooted up.

Jeremiah 1:10

See, I have this day set thee over the nations and over the kingdoms, to root out, and to pull down, and to destroy, and to throw down, to build, and to plant.

Matthew 17:20

And Jesus said unto them, Because of your unbelief: for verily I say unto you, If ye have faith as a grain of mustard seed, ye shall say unto this mountain, Remove hence to yonder place; and it shall remove; and nothing shall be impossible unto you.

Luke 10:19

Behold, I give unto you power to tread on serpents and scorpions, and over all the power of the enemy: and nothing shall by any means hurt you.

Psalms 91

He that dwelleth in the secret place of the most High shall abide under the shadow of the Almighty.

I will say of the Lord, He is my refuge and my fortress: my God; in him will I trust.

Surely he shall deliver thee from the snare of the fowler, and from the noisome pestilence.

He shall cover thee with his feathers, and under his wings shalt thou trust: his truth shall be thy shield and buckler.

Thou shalt not be afraid for the terror by night; nor for the arrow that flieth by day;

Nor for the pestilence that walketh in darkness; nor for the destruction that wasteth at noonday.

A thousand shall fall at thy side, and ten thousand at thy right hand; but it shall not come nigh thee.

Only with thine eyes shalt thou behold and see the reward of the wicked.

Because thou hast made the Lord, which is my refuge, even the most High, thy habitation;

There shall no evil befall thee, neither shall any plague come nigh thy dwelling.

For he shall give his angels charge over thee, to keep thee in all thy ways.

They shall bear thee up in their hands, lest thou dash thy foot against a stone.

Thou shalt tread upon the lion and adder: the young lion and the dragon shalt thou trample under feet.

Because he hath set his love upon me, therefore will I deliver him: I will set him on high, because he hath known my name.

He shall call upon me, and I will answer him: I will be with him in trouble; I will deliver him, and honour him.

With long life will I satisfy him, and shew him my salvation.

Psalms 27

The Lord is my light and my salvation; whom shall I fear? the Lord is the strength of my life; of whom shall I be afraid?

When the wicked, even mine enemies and my foes, came upon me to eat up my flesh, they stumbled and fell.

Though an host should encamp against me, my heart shall not fear: though war should rise against me, in this will I be confident.

One thing have I desired of the Lord, that will I seek after; that I may dwell in the house of the Lord all the days of my life, to behold the beauty of the Lord, and to enquire in his temple.

For in the time of trouble he shall hide me in his pavilion: in the secret of his tabernacle shall he hide me; he shall set me up upon a rock.

And now shall mine head be lifted up above mine enemies round about me: therefore will I offer in his tabernacle sacrifices of joy; I will sing, yea, I will sing praises unto the Lord.

Hear, O Lord, when I cry with my voice: have mercy also upon me, and answer me.

When thou saidst, Seek ye my face; my heart said unto thee, Thy face, Lord, will I seek.

Hide not thy face far from me; put not thy servant away in anger: thou hast been my help; leave me not, neither forsake me, O God of my salvation.

When my father and my mother forsake me, then the Lord will take me up.

Teach me thy way, O Lord, and lead me in a plain path, because of mine enemies.

Deliver me not over unto the will of mine enemies: for false witnesses are risen up against me, and such as breathe out cruelty.

I had fainted, unless I had believed to see the goodness of the Lord in the land of the living.

Wait on the Lord: be of good courage, and he shall strengthen thine heart: wait, I say, on the Lord.

From A Caterpillar To A Butterfly

Poem By Tupac Shakur

The Rose That Grew From Concrete

Did you hear about the rose that grew

from a crack in the concrete?

Proving nature's law is wrong it

learned to walk with out having feet.

Funny it seems, but by keeping it's dreams,

it learned to breathe fresh air.

Long live the rose that grew from concrete

when no one else ever cared.

He'll Make A Way

Poem By Sierra Stephenson

I know sometimes life gets hard but it's okay,
all you gotta do is a little bit of faith

Just keep on pressing and keep on praying,
declare and decreeing peace is in the making;

No problem too big nor too small for
my God who is in control of it all

My God My God the savior of the day I live
in your will and always praise your name

No matter the time or the day our
Father will always make a way!

Their will be some dark days but many brighter
days so keep your head up and never give up faith

The battles that we face he fights them each
day God oh God I praise your name; I'll
praise your name for the rest of my days

Coming From A Dark Place

I came from a very dark place after my mother passed away. I went down the wrong path, the path of destruction! It was like being stuck in a sunken hole with no way out. I didn't know how deep I was in and the things that I had begun to do were out of who I was before. I had lost sight of who I was and didn't know who I had become. Growing up around friends and family that didn't speak life over you as a teen but only word curses. I was told I wasn't going to amount up to anything, I was accused of having sex before I had even started and thats exactly what made me become curisous. There were so many things I faced because I had no sense of direction. At this time I was only 14 years old surrounded by all adult's. I was led astray by people that were family and friends of family not realizing I was being manipulated and used because I was young and vulnerable. Taught how to reel men in and have relations with no ties or feeling's being involved.. I was the youngest one and was used to getting men for my cousins because they had already been in the streets way before me. I wasn't shown the correct way to live. I wasn't taught about the things that I should've known at that age. It had gotten so bad to where I had been physically, mentally and verbally abused, kidnapped, mistreated, misled, misguided, degraded, trapped in a spirit I had no way of getting away from. Going from pillow to post, riding the city bus after school with nowhere to go, being kicked out of family homes because their husband or wives didn't want me there even though these were the same people my mother helped out and would've given the shirt off her back. It was a point in life when I used to carry bags down the street because I had nowhere to put my clothes. I didn't have a choice at this point but to do what I needed to survive because I wasn't taught the real, the right way to live life.. I had lived with a few people but all they saw was a check because I had received survivor benefits when my mother passed away. Once that was gone, so was I. It's been many nights I've had to deal with nasty homes and attitudes just to have a place to lay my head. I've laid on floors, couches and even dealt with men... Being touched when you don't want to but you have no place to lay your head is the worst feeling ever. I would never wish this kind of situation on anyone in the world.. I lost self respect, my dignity and righteousness during this time in my life... I couldn't call on no one because the few choices I made in the beginning of my life made them look at me differently... I had gotten sick of living my life to please and keep my family happy. I had never stepped out and truly lived for my own happiness and in the beginning of this terrible transformation I thought that's what I had begun to do not knowing I was running my life. I didn't have my older siblings to teach me or show me the way. Once my mom passed away it was like they forgot they had younger siblings and lived their lives. We all grew up in the same household our whole lives. Us 4 were all we knew no matter what the situation was. We could argue and fight and my mom would always tell us how when she left this earth we'll only have each other but I couldn't even see that at this time. I was a broken young girl, my father wasn't in the picture because of his habits and the things he was faced with. In the midst of it all I knew things would get better, the dark days would begin to get brighter and my hurt would become joy again.. It would just take time to get past this phase. I've always known in the back of my mind that God was with me and I wasn't meant for the life that I had chosen to live.

Stepping Into The light

I've always known that God has called me to be someone in life but I didn't know what... I had felt this way since I was a little girl, many days I went to tell my sister that I was special and she'd look confused not really understanding what I was meaning. I believe God sent my son to save my life because I wasn't paying any attention to the things that mattered. When I conceived my first child I had stopped hanging out for a while, I stopped smoking, doing drugs and drinking. God started to align my life for the things he wanted for me. I had started spending more time alone to get me in order. It was like God was trying to tell me something. I started to seek him more and noticed I was being blessed. He had been there all along but was just waiting on me to open my heart and call out to him. I backslid a few times. It wasn't until my son turned 2 years old that I started my walk with God but I was a lukewarm, a faint believer and started to notice how I only really called on Jesus when I was in need or trouble passed me by. I began going back to Church and fell off again. It was like a toxic relationship, back and forth.. off and on type of situation... Every time The Lord took me back with open arms... Then a few years later I began to have a relationship with this woman; I believe at this point God was upset because he had sent a message for me to a Prophet that I had started to join on facebook live a few months previously. The first time he prophesied to me was April 10th 2020 saying God is breathing in my direction. The lord said something has been fighting me eternally and he's breathing on it and blowing things away that don't belong in my life. He's causing a new day and a new me and anywhere in my life that enemy has caused me to have to wait for the Lord to come for me ... He heard the Lord say he's coming for me around the midnight hour and I'll remember that he is God and beside him is no other and I'll know that he is real. At the midnight hour he's vindicating me. He said that the fire is going to burn and it'll burn anything that doesn't belong and is going to be burnt away. The reason I felt the lord gave him that message for me is because I was taught wrong that you're not supposed to fear God since he is for us and not against us. That whole night I was worried and scared, crying, praying on my knees and repenting for things I was doing and have done in my life. As I laid down it was close to midnight and my back began to get really hot and I couldn't shake the feeling because it kept going... I couldn't understand what was going on but then something else happened, I was looking around my room and I felt the spirit of the angels protecting my home and watching me like if they were guarding me until the lord came to visit... not even two minutes later I felt if my spirit was being lifting out of my body so I jumped out of bed and went to my living room with my brother. I let him listen to the video of the prophet and he got scared so I tried smoking a cigarette and the Holy Spirit spoke to me and said don't light that... I lit it anyway because I was so nervous.. Then I began to get up for something to drink and he said again don't get up or your knees will get weak. I couldn't even get up. In my heart I wanted to run out that door but there was no place to hide from God.! I stayed in the living room on the couch not trying to fall asleep but the POWER OF THE HOLY SPIRIT is so Powerful that it knocked me right out... The whole time I had been scared to fall asleep because I thought I was going to die... My brother told me I placed my hand on his forehead and began to pray for him as I slept. I remember being asleep and speaking to God it was dark but I saw a white outline of a face... I didn't see his true face, just an image. I had promised that I wasn't going to deal with women anymore and how I was going to help my brother try to stay healthy and how I wasn't going to get plastic surgery. The next morning I woke up to many missed calls from the girl I had been dealing with. She said that in her dream I had cheated on her and she was devastated, not knowing the encounter I had with God last night .. I knew that was the end of us...! August 21st 2020 was the second time he prophesied that The lord said no longer will I cry about who walked out of my life for he is bringing the right individuals to me and even as he began to do that he said this should be a hour I began to see things as I've never seen it before. God said I am a dreamer. I am about to dream my way out, I've been in a place where everything I've been through I have always been able to dream my way out. Dream a new dream, dream a bigger dream, dream a stratigrect dream. He said as I dream my way out he is preparing the way for me, he's going to open the right doors, bring the right connections and put me in the right environment. The sound of grace is upon my life and he has stopped the attack on my family and has stopped the attack on my mind...! At this time I knew that God had been trying to get me to realize that he has something major for me to do in the crazy world we live in. It was my time to step up and answer the call! In January 2021 I started my first fast. It lasted for 5 days just liquid , February 2021 I started my second fast that lasted for 10 days and I was able to receive my breakthrough.. September 2021 I started my 3rd fast and this time I was pregnant... I was looking for God to come visit me in my dreams like he normally does but he had something different in mind. It wasn't dreams he had begun to speak through my spirit and I also was able to hear from the Holy Spirit.

Letting Go &; Letting God

Letting go was the hardest thing I had to deal with because I was so used to leaning on my own understanding and not Gods, I had gotten so used to doing things my way, providing for myself and not having to answer to anyone. When someone says let go and let God you start to think what anyone would; It's easier said than done right.? Same thing I thought. It's a challenge that you have to be ready for because in the back of our minds we always go back to the comfortable thought process or the way we're used to doing things. I had kept doing these exact thing's believing I could change things myself when in reality I couldn't. That goes back to letting stuff be when it's out of your control. There were days when I wanted to give up because I didn't see any progress in my situation. It wasn't easy, some days were harder than others. I couldn't get past all the pain that I once hid deep inside. I had begun to oppress my thoughts and memories, thinking it'll get better. I didn't realize it was only getting worse. Late nights, early mornings the thought would start to resurface my mind. That's when I knew something had to be done about the things I'd been experiencing. It's been many nights I've cried, vented to friends and family. I've gone to speak with doctors and had been prescribed medication, they diagnosed me with anxiety and depression but that still didn't help. It wasn't until I seeked God about it. He had all the answers to the problems I faced. He gave me understanding through this because I had gone through my life trying to figure out why some many bad things were happening to me. I had begun to think It was my fault. The way I had been treated and the things people decided to do to me. The rejection I felt from not being accepted by people. The way I was treated when I had become accepted. I felt if I was never good enough because growing up I was the one that didn't fit in but tried to fit in. I didn't have many friends and the ones I thought were my friend used, abused and mistreated me for being me.. It had begun to make me feel as if I had to change who God had created me to be just to have a social life.. That's when the identity crisis came because at that point I didn't know who I was. Trying to fit in for so long I became someone else. It was time for me to live in my truth and do some soul searching. I had to pray to the lord to see what and who I was called to be because I had no idea.While in that identity crisis and you start to see who you are, you'll eventually find your likes and dislikes, things you wanted to be growing up as a child, you'll began to remember who you truly are. In order to let go of the pain I felt I had to first let go of the pain I've caused myself, it all starts within. As an adult I can't go around blaming people for the things that have happened in my life. At some point we have to stand up and take responsibility for some of the thing's. It's up to you to make that change and move on for the better, nobody is going to be there to hold your hand in the process. That's why it's important to lean on God's understanding and not own our... This took me many years of continually bumping my head, falling and getting back up just to try it again.. the fight is never over. At this stage it's only the beginning of an ever lasting fight .. The good thing is that we won't be alone once we let go and let God, now the fight is his ... it's been his we just took on the battle ourselves not realizing it. Thinking we could win the victory alone when we face things it's normally not in the flesh it's in the spirit once I figured out it was never people hurting me it was the spirit on them and within them.. Is when the burnden rolled off my back. Thinking back all this time the battle was never mine. I had been attacked by the same spirit that was on these individuals. I had spent many days in a dark room, a dark quiet place, worshiping, praising and praying to the Lord for strength and peace... No matter how much I tried letting go it was like something was trying to hold me back from what God was wanting to do with me in my life at this season. There would often be times where the enemy would start placing things in my mind to remind me of my past and try to bring me back to that dark whole that God had gotten me out of. The devil would start trying to send a spirit of discouragement, resentment, fear, confusion, just to distract me from being able to release that stronghold, he was upset. Once we allow the Lord to work within us that's when the attacks begin. No one has ever said it'll be easy, it's going to be a fight against your flesh and spirit because the flesh has its own desires but God's desires for us are deeper, better, healther, it's life and not death.. God will use the same ones that spoke down on your name and mistreated you to pay you, respect and honor you. In the end he will promote you right in the face of your enemies. He will fill your plate up while they starve from being so wicked to you. The thing's you went through could also be the reason you get to where God has called you to be but in order to make it that far you first have to allow God to take over the problems you face because they were his from the start. The time is now sisters in Christ.. Do whatever you have to do to let go of that hurt that's hindering you from being where you are destined to be

Acceptance & Forgiveness

Coming from a place where I accepted the wrong thing's and thought I forgave everything because I've always wanted to see the good in every situation but all along it was wrong. I was wrong... I wasn't accepting what I should be and forgiving the correct way.. If you're wondering if there is a right and wrong way to forgive the answer is yes, you can say I forgive you but in your heart and spirit you really don't. See ladies it's deeper than the eye can see and the hand can touch, the flesh can't meet because it's deceiving but what it doesn't like is the Holy Spirit...! For many years I had been taught wrong by my peers, friends and family... Words mean nothing if you don't believe and have faith to back you up. I just learned how to forgive the right way, God sat me down for a few months until I learned how to accept the thing's I had no control over and how to forgive myself for the thing's I took myself through and the thing's that I should've never accepted. Then I was able to start the process of forgiveness in others for the trauma that I was dealt... It took years for me to understand the process of acceptance and be able to really forgive. It's so much that comes with that. The things that took place happened because it was already written in the book. God wants us to use the pain for power. Some become bitter but that only kills you spiritually. I didn't know the things I held on to from when I was 6 years old were still haunting me in adulthood. If we don't deal with these things it becomes detrimental to our life's purpose and we will be held back from what God has for us. These things are a part of our testimony and others need to hear how you got through your situation because there are so many people that need uplifting, encouraging words to keep them pushing through the storm they're faced with each day. I had to dig real deep and press into the Holy Spirit, cry, write, pray, sing, laugh, confront the situation at hand, start my grieving process. It was time to let go of the things that weren't good for me. It took for me to accept and forgive myself the hurt I put me through, being accountable for my own actions, to get through it all. I couldn't blame people for all of my problems and the things I've experienced because I also put myself in situations. It started with self forgiveness and accepting things that were unacceptable. Once I did that and started to live in my truth, I felt the biggest release of me, mentally, physically, emotionally and spiritually. If I didn't turn to God, not only would I continue to go through the storm without any shelter but I also wouldn't be able to move to the next season... the next level of what God has for my life and the things he's desired for my life's purpose... He'll turn our pain into purpose... our tears of sorrow into tears of joy...

Romans 15:7 (KJV)

Wherefore receive ye one another, as Christ also received us to the glory of God.

John 1:12 (KJV)

But as many as received him, to them gave he power to become the sons of God, even to them that believe on his name.

Matthew 6:14 (KJV)

For if ye forgive men their trespasses, your heavenly Father will also forgive you

Luke 6:27 (KJV)

But I say unto you which hear, Love your enemies, do good to them which hate you,

The Power of Healing

The process of healing is one of the toughest seasons to go through because you have to deal with the past trauma and face situations you once feared. It's definitely not easy. There are many triggers for me like snow, the holiday season and certain music. In order to receive a healed heart you have to allow God to come in and perform surgery, strip you clean of the things that were weighing you down. Sometimes things get into our hearts without us even realizing what's taking place because we didn't protect ourselves. Our hearts are not only created for us to live and love but it is a vessel for God to use. I'm not only speaking about the physical heart that beats in your chest but the heart of your mind, body and soul. God wants us to evaluate what we are filled with so we could be renewed. The way we can begin to do it is by opening your heart and mouth, accepting Jesus as your Lord and savior, building a relationship with God, Jesus and The Holy Spirit through the bible. I'm not speaking about religion, I am

speaking on a spiritual divine connection. Learning who God truly is and not focusing on what he can do for you because that all comes depending on your walk. God will begin to move in you and your life like never before. That is why he is called our provider because he provides more than our little brains could imagination. God sent Jesus to walk the earth for 33 years to pave the way for us to follow his lead, he is our Lord and Savior he died on the cross for our sins and God sent The Holy Spirit to be active in your everyday life never leaving our side all we have to do is seek him, and he'll be there.. No we all may not be able to hear him or even know when he is around but that comes with faith and how much you believe. In this walk you can't be lukewarm and think you'll be healed by the blood of

Jesus and the power of God. My question to you is how strong is your faith? That right there determines a lot in your life and the path your life will take. You'll know when you're healed because your heart will feel full of love and empty of pain and sorrow. You will have peace within and a warmth feeling... It'll be a big weight being lifted and peace within. You won't feel heavy and like you're carrying many burdens. You won't need to seek confirmation because this will be a feeling like no other. No matter how long ago the Lord has healed you, that hurt, the enemy will always try to bring it back up and throw it in your face but it is up to you to leave it your rear view and choose not to look back. During this time you will be attacked and the enemy as we all know comes for three things and that's to steal, kill and destroy. You have the power to stay protected as long as you stay covered in the will and word of god. Knowing the power of prayers for protection will help you on this journey ahead because the deeper your walk the more warfare you'll receive. Don't be faint, don't be led by fear or confusion for those are not the spirit of the Lord. Make sure you also watch who you allow in your life and in your home. Watch what you hear, see and speak. Many people will even try to bring up your past, people get mad when they can't touch who you are because they'll be stuck on who you used to be. They don't realize that with the strength of God anything is possible. Just remember to keep the strong faith, pray with authority, walk boldly in who God has called you to be and go when he says go, stop when he says stop, speak when he says speak, and always ask The Holy Spirit for guidance.

Isaiah 26:3 (KJV)

Thou wilt keep him in perfect peace, whose mind is stayed on thee: because he trusteth in thee.

John 14:27 (KJV)

Peace I leave with you, my peace I give unto you: not as the world giveth, give I unto you. Let not your heart be troubled, neither let it be afraid.

Revelation 21:4 (KJV)

And God shall wipe away all tears from their eyes; and there shall be no more death, neither sorrow, nor crying, neither shall there be any more pain: for the former things are passed away.

Humility

I can honestly say that I never knew I had a problem with being humble because growing up I've always been a caregiver at heart and took care of close friends and family. For some reason I had kept everyone's need a priority besides my own. That was a strength but a weakness I noticed. One thing I struggled with was becoming more humble when it came to certain situations like things I couldn't change or when I was on the next person's time. During the time I was in my wilderness season the lord had sat me down and humbled me real quickly. I grew to learn patience for the things I once didn't have them for. I've always spoken my mind and been very bold but respectful. I had begun learning how to speak when spoken to or how to not speak at all because everything doesn't deserve a response. Not all actions need a reaction. God had dealt with me a lot during this time because there were a few things I thought I had under control that I had no control over and that was the problem. I was so focused on caring for the issues myself instead of allowing God to take care of them and provide for my needs, whether it was meantally, physically, emotionally, financially or spiritually. I wasn't humble in these areas enough for the Lord to work within my life. I did things on my own because if they weren't done in a timely manner I would lose my patience. In this past time it didn't dawn on me to ask the lord for help and if I was doing things the correct way. I could say sometimes I was a bit selfish. I have always tried looking at things on the brighter side for the most part. I mean we are all human and no one is perfect. During the summer of 2021 I had been through so much within 3 months, It was like God was saying daughter be still. Everything happened at once, my car had gotten impounded, I purchased a new car only to have much trouble with it so I sold it. I got into a car crash and I also was experiencing really bad headaches, dizziness, being light headed and fatigue all this occurring while being pregnant. I wasn't able to work for months due to the crash and dizzy spells I was having, but God had better plans for me even though I didn't understand that in the beginning. It took a few weeks to realize what had been taking place. In this time while I was going through this process I learned to trust in God, I was able to accept these things that had occurred. I was able to appreciate what I did have and believed that it was enough for me and my child. I became more humble and found what grace was. I believe these things took place to get me prepared for greater things. God has started to show up more and more. My faith grew, and my strength in the lord also grew. I was able to sit back and allow the lord to work out my kinks and wrinkles. Now I am able to evaluate situations I am faced with in life when they happen because I was being prepared for life and it's mishaps

1 Peter 5:6 (KJV)

Humble yourselves therefore under the mighty hand of God, that he may exalt you in due time.

James 4:6 (KJV)

But he giveth more grace. Wherefore he saith, God resisteth the proud, but giveth grace unto the humble.

Proverbs 15:33 (KJV)

The fear of the Lord is the instruction of wisdom; and before honour is humility.

The Road To Recovery

The road to recovery is just like the road to success, it gets lonely but in the end you'll have much joy deep within. It's not that you're alone because God is always with you, It's letting go of the worldly ways, it's pride, it's non morals and ways. The things the crowd do and say are the actions of being a non believer. Living in a world that's full of corruption but being a part of it's solutions, being the light in the darkest places and leading the sheep to it's shepherd. On this earth we all have a purpose and a job to do... The question is when God calls are you going to answer? Most of the time we'll either miss the call or not hear it because we're not hearing or seeing the signs God has given us. This was something I had been afraid of for many years because I kept being pulled back but by the grace God had on my life he closed those old doors. Now one thing about the Lord is... when he closes a door nothing or no one can reopen them. It not only saved my life but I was able to hear the phone ring. Just know if he could do it for me he can do it for you and anyone else that's ready to say YES! That's it sister.. That's God's favorite word and it'll eventually be yours because we know that our father will never steer us wrong.! Sometimes we might not understand the things he's guiding us to do but it'll all make sense later down the line. Our lives are like puzzle pieces. God will give us a few things to start with first and once we complete those tasks he'll continue to keep adding on pieces. Once you see it coming together then you'll realize it's some real work getting done... God will never promote you without equipping you for the job he's called you to work on and the positions he's giving you.. Whatever you do, don't move faster than the Lord because it'll not only cause you to fall out of alignment but it'll also cause you to delay yourself to the promises of God... Yes God has promised all of his children land, the land of our ancestors and not only that but he's promised us many other things and whatever it is he's promised you just make sure you don't forfeit because it's possible to happen if your heart isn't in the right place make sure to be intentional with everything you do. let's not be obedient because of the promises of God but because of who he is. When taking action in the things God has planned for our lives we grow exhausted and overwhelmed if not going back to our power source which is the Lord for strength and to rest in his presence. He'll be able to restore you when needed, giving you that freshly renewed spirit and energy. God calls us to stewardship because there is much labor but not many laborers, it's all about your good works and bringing people to Christ. The lord had dealt with me one night and gave me a few words. They were reconciliation and resurrection. I believe he was telling me that our relationship was being mended and he was blessing me with salvation being saved from death, meaning death of the spirit because the enemy had been

trying to kill me spiritually in this past year but the lord had taken his hands right off of me and my life. The relationship I worked hard for paid off because I was not only saved, restored, and favored but he also blessed me with the Holy Spirit and being able to discern the voice of God. That morning I woke up feeling rejuvenated and full of love, life and peace within my mind, body and soul. All you have to do is be ready when he calls no matter how big the tasks may seem at hand, go through the rough and tough patches because it'll all be worth it... The light will shine bright at the end of the tunnel and you'll be able to lead others to that light the same way you were led.

2 Corinthians 9:6-7 (KJV)

But this I say, He which soweth sparingly shall reap also sparingly; and he which soweth bountifully shall reap also bountifully.

Every man according as he purposeth in his heart, so let him give; not grudgingly, or of necessity: for God loveth a cheerful giver.

Ephesians 4:32 (KJV)

And be ye kind one to another, tenderhearted, forgiving one another, even as God for Christ's sake hath forgiven you.

2 Corinthians 5:17 (KJV)

Therefore if any man be in Christ, he is a new creature: old things are passed away; behold, all things are become new.

John 11:25-26 (KJV)

Jesus said unto her, I am the resurrection, and the life: he that believeth in me, though he were dead, yet shall he live.

And whosoever liveth and believeth in me shall never die. Believest thou this?

John 3:16-17 (KJV)

For God so loved the world, that he gave his only begotten Son, that whosoever believeth in him should not perish, but have everlasting life.

For God sent not his Son into the world to condemn the world; but that the world through him might be saved.

Redemption

Redemption is the act of being saved by yours truly, I mean he's not just saving our lives but he's also saving our love, and peace that we have within him. He's saving the generations next to come, giving them a chance at the promised land he's giving you. The only way to be saved is through growing a relationship and accepting Jesus Christ as our Lord and savior. I don't know how many times I've said this but I can't stress it enough... There are many test's and seasons you'll have to go through and just because you have been redeemed doesn't mean this is it. It gets deeper, your relationship with God needs to be intament. Trials and tribulations still stand. It won't be easy but it'll be better because you know the Lord is with you every step of the way guiding you out of the desert, Knowing that Jesus died on the cross for our sins just to save us and keep us clean by the blood. There is also a price to pay, you have to allow God to kill what's on the inside of you because it's taking up space for him to use you as the vessel that you are. The worldly thought process you have, the attitude, the way you act as a person, the way you carry yourself down to the way you dress...! God wants it all.. He wants to know that you'll be able to be who he has called you to be and at your best ... Our father wants nothing but the best for us. We have to surrender to our ways and submit to him..! Many things are dead in this season you're in and now is the time to let it go... I'm sure God has been giving many red flags and signs that things aren't meant for you but you have been living in denial and ignoring them thinking it'll all work out but deep down inside you know that there's no point in giving life to a dead situation whether it's a relationship or not.. Inorder for our Father to bring forth life into our lives we have to die to old things and ways, throw away things that no longer serve a purpose. Having crazy faith, believing faith I mean saving faith, and standing on the word of God will have you moving in boldness.! It's important for you to trust and believe, not that but believe and know that the Lord Jesus Christ is your Lord and Savior and he died on the cross for your sins. Are you a true believer..? because there's no time for being lukewarm, backsliding, half stepping and faint living.. It's all or nothing when it comes down to the walk with God. As for me I have accepted my position as a servant to God; everyday I look forward to seeing what God has planned out for the day because I know the way he moves and the things he is capable of. When you get to this point in your walk just know you are cleansed of all dirt and sin, your debt has been collected and God has allowed you to regain the possessions you once let go of..! The promise he's giving you is yours but it's up to you whether or not you'll keep following the way, it's so easy to become sidetracked and at this time it's no reason to beauces nothing is more important that staying in obedience with God, staying in position, if you move the wrong way you're bound to get lost or miss out on what's just for you, so go through the process and be patient knowing he'll never leave nor forsake you.. He's nothing like the people that neglected and abused you.. Our Father is a man of his words and never lies.. For redemption the cost is obedience and sacrifice.

Colossians 1:20-22 (KJV)

And, having made peace through the blood of his cross, by him to reconcile all things unto himself; by him, I say, whether they be things in earth, or things in heaven.

And you, that were sometime alienated and enemies in your mind by wicked works, yet now hath he reconciled

In the body of his flesh through death, to present you holy and unblameable and unreproveable in his sight

Romans 3:24 (KJV)

Being justified freely by his grace through the redemption that is in Christ Jesus

Epilogue

God's grace and mercy

The mercy and grace God has blessed each of with is undeserved, have fallen short each day, but he's still with us cheering us on to keep going. The Lord blesses us with new grace and mercy every morning we wake up. We don't give God enough praise and thanks for these beautiful blessings he bestowed upon our lives. the Lord is so beautiful, he is so gentle with us, he's so loving, he's so sweet, he's so forgiving, God is so faithful. He loves us more than anyone could ever love us. God will never leave nor forsake us.. He will never let us go.. We tend to leave God side when it gets tough.. It shouldn't be like that because he wouldn't do that to us. God deserves loyalty, he deserves unconditional love like he gives us.Through tough times, though the rain and storms God deserves our best no matter what we're faced within this lifetime. We can be very ungrateful when God doesn't have to give us life,breath or love but he does. It's time to be more intentional when spending time with Our Father. Lets not continue to sin and live wickedly because God gives us grace and mercy because if it's taken advantage of he will take it away and nobody wants that warth and smoke of the father so it's time to step up and do right. The lord had begun to deal with me about fasting. I did a liquid fast, just water. He has sent people to help me on my journey to being delivered and to grow a stronger relationship with him., To be healed so I can be used the way he needs me to be. I was delivered from the spirit of Herod and an Echo Spirit. They wanted to kill me, they also wanted me to hate my children. The spirits wanted to drive me crazy mentally. Someone has been practicing witchcraft on me. I had gone on this app called clubhouse and this lady pinged me into this room. When I went into the room for this lady's birthday gathering my flesh wanted me to get out of the room but my spirit wanted me to stay so I obeyed my spirit. After I had spoken out about them helping my spirit be uplifted; after that I began to weep. This lady spoke to me saying that postpartum depression was trying to attach to me. There also were the demonic spirits, they had a rope tied around my neck and ankles. This man had just come into the room and prayed for me, spoke life into me and then dispatched the angels from heaven to come and cut me loose. I coughed and was choking.. That was the spirits releasing me, after that happened my neck and ankles felt free. It was from a soul tie that I had from an ex - partner. That next night the Lord began to heal my body and internally, I woke up the next day and felt completely new, fresh. I can't really express the way I felt because I have never felt it before. It was a calm feeling, I was completely at peace within myself and it was something different. The spirit of confusion tried to jump off on me because the Lord had given me a peace of mind and that made the enemy mad. the Lord healed my heart, before this I couldn't feel anything in my heart. It felt like I had a heavy empty heart that had a chain and lock on it. I was very uncomfortable because I know I love the Lord and He loves me but I couldn't feel anything, and that's because the love of God is by action not by words; it's the way we teach each other and the way we obey the Father. The enemy wanted me to feel condemnation; but the Lord gave me a word and he will always let us know when we're coming up short. Even though you get delivered doesn't mean that you won't have those attacks trying to come back up. It's still a fight to stay delivered and walk this thing out solid and strong. After everything I been though i woudn't change a thing because It's made me who I am today. I wouldn't be able to tell this story or about how good God has been to me through it all. No matter what I felt like, no matter what it looked like, God was still by my side and never left me, even when I did things that he didn't approve of he loved me enough to clean me up and use my pain and turn it into purpose. God recieves all of the glory for the woman I am today and for the great sucess that is in store for my future. I give God all the praise aand life his name high because he is mighty... Nobody could've brought me out of that deep dark place is was in but the most high and I want to publicly give him what he truly deserve. I couldn't have done it without his gracy and mery. I say to you brother and sister stay in prayer. Buil a bond with the Lord and know through the storm Our Father will bring you out untouched. May the Lord be with you all.